How **Spending** and **Saving** Affect You

John Strazzabosco

ROSEN
PUBLISHING®

New York

Published in 2013 by The Rosen Publishing Group, Inc.
29 East 21st Street, New York, NY 10010

Library of Congress Cataloging-in-Publication Data

Strazzabosco, John.
How spending and saving affect you/John Strazzabosco.—1st ed.
    p. cm.—(Your economic future)
Includes bibliographical references and index.
ISBN 978-1-4488-8344-8 (library binding)
1. Saving and investment—United States. 2. Consumption
(Economics)—United States. I. Title.
 HC110.S3.S83 2013
 339.4'30973—dc23

                                                              2012017552

Manufactured in the United States of America

CPSIA Compliance Information: Batch #W13YA: For further information, contact Rosen Publishing, New York, New York, at 1-800-237-9932.

Contents

A stroll through the mall brings many tempting, yet nonessential, products into view. The stores do all they can to make their products appealing, but it is up to consumers to make the responsible decision of whether to spend or save.

Introduction

How we spend or save our money some-times brings on a heated family discussion. One day you plead for a flat-screen television for the family, and the expressions brought to your parents' faces suggest that is not going to happen.

When you ask why not, your father begins to talk about his retirement plan. From your father's tone and body language, you get the idea that he would make the television purchase if he could. He doesn't like disappointing you. That's clear. He explains that money that would go to a tele-vision would be much better used elsewhere. If he invests in his retirement plan at work, called a 401(k), he and your mom would be on track to retire when planned.

He elaborates on how a 401(k) works. Your dad is seizing the moment, giving you a lesson on how spending and saving affect you. Saving requires deferred gratification, putting off a purchase into the future. On the one hand, you badly want that television now. On the other hand, money put into a retirement account tends to grow over time. After many years, the money he would have spent on a television would have grown sizably.

This lesson makes you wonder. You recently received $20 for your birthday, and it suddenly occurs to you that you will soon be forced to make a similar choice: spend or save your $20? What would make you choose to save your $20 instead of spending it, or vice versa?

Chapter 1

On the National Level

You may not realize it, but the ways that countries around the world spend and save their money have a great impact on you. Each country's way of spending and saving is important. Some countries are big spenders, and some are big savers.

All nations participate in the world economy, and each country impacts the others to a certain degree. This is part of what we call globalization. As author Greg Ip says in *The Little Book of Economics*, "Globalization is exerting an often hidden influence, the way a distant planet's gravitational pull alters another planet's orbit." So one country's economy might drag another's up or down. Even when you follow good spending and saving practices, things can go wrong. But exactly how does it affect you?

Today, many of the products Americans consume are exported from China by sea and air, which keeps costs lower than if they were made in America.

A Tale of Two Countries

We start with a comparison of the world's two major economic powers, which have very different ideas on how to run their economy: the United States and China. At the time of this writing, the United States is the most dominant economic power in the world. Spending is a big part of it. China is the second most dominant economic power in the world. Saving is a big part of the Chinese economy.

Economic success stories can result from radically different approaches. We'll look now at how this spending and saving affect the relationship between the two superpowers…and ultimately you.

During the Iraq War, the United States required massive funding to finance its armed forces. Yet where would the money come from? One possible source was taxes. The decision was not to raise

Raising Money with Bonds

The way one country invests in another is normally done through the sale of bonds. For example, if America needs money and China has the funds available, Chinese investors send those funds to America and America issues a bond, a financial instrument that serves as an I.O.U., or something borrowed. In this case, the bonds were issued by the U.S. Treasury.

U.S. Treasury bonds are often just called Treasuries. Treasuries not only pay interest each year from America to whoever holds the bonds, but they are also worth the purchase price paid for each bond. When the bondholder later

Savings bonds allow governments to raise capital from its citizens. A form of I.O.U, bonds are sold to members of the public, who get back their money at a later date with interest.

cashes in those bonds, each investor gets his or her money back, plus the interest due.

However, a problem potentially arises. If China holds the bonds, and after a year the interest on the bond is due, what happens if America doesn't have the funds to pay off that interest? The owing party—in this case, America—is said to be in default. For a country, the bad reputation of becoming the defaulting party could hurt its ability to borrow money in the future, among other issues. A bad reputation might cause a whole country's economic system to suffer.

Therefore, bond sales do come with risks. As author Ip says, though, "The U.S. Treasury bond market is to the world... a safe place to store cash you need in a hurry." In other words, a country can depend on getting back its investment, plus interest, when buying U.S. Treasuries whenever it wants.

For that matter, you might also someday decide to invest in Treasuries or other government bonds, like U.S. savings bonds, if you wanted a safe place to keep your cash for a while and earn some interest.

taxes on U.S. citizens. However, where else could America find funding for its military?

The United States found one resource in China. Since the Chinese are savers, China had money available to lend. So China made cash investments in U.S. Treasury bonds so that America could finance its war in Iraq.

How might that sale of U.S. Treasuries to China during the Iraq War years affect you and your savings? There are billions upon billions of dollars in interest payments due to China for the bonds the country bought. Additionally, when the bonds themselves are cashed in by China, that money will have to be raised from somewhere in America to pay China back. If no means are available, the U.S. government might decide to get the money by raising taxes. If your parents' income taxes went up, they would have less money to save or spend, and that flat-screen television might be delayed for a while longer than they hoped.

National Budgets

You might wonder how America became a nation of spenders while China became a nation of savers. You might also question how this affects you. Government regulations play a big factor in our spending and saving. As the leading consumer of goods in the world, America imports many products from other countries. The U.S. government enforces fewer regulations

The Great Recession led to a nationwide increase in home foreclosures. Part of the reason for the collapse in the housing market was overspending on homes.

on business so that spending is encouraged, which in turn strengthens America's economy.

That's not to say that enormous problems don't occur at times. The recent Great Recession wreaked havoc in the United States and the global financial world. Normally the term "recession" is the name for a downturn in the economy that lasts for several months. The Great Recession, however, lasted several years, from 2006 to 2009. It led many people to lose their jobs.

Gross Domestic Product

To more quickly measure the state of any nation's economy, economists use a number called the gross domestic product, or GDP. The number allows them to compare economies even when the countries are quite different in many ways. For instance, each country has its own currency, and currency is valued differently from one country to the next, and so comparisons can be difficult to make.

Also, as we've seen, some countries are spenders and others are savers, some sell bonds and some buy them, and many different characteristics exist from one country to the next.

The GDP calculation is one way to create a level playing field and more easily compare one country's economy with another's. It takes into account a country's consumer spending, business investments, government spending, and exports minus its imports.

Meanwhile, recall from our earlier example, if your mom lost a job during the Great Recession, not only were your chances of getting a flat-screen television reduced, but also those of your getting a smartphone, skateboard, and perhaps drum lessons. That's just another example of a nation's spending and savings habits affecting you.

The U.S. government policy tends to be more hands-off with the economy, letting it drive itself, innovate, and make its own rules. On the other hand, the Chinese government enforces strict regulations so that saving, rather than spending, is encouraged. Saving causes manufacturers to lower the price of goods so that potential customers might want to buy. Low prices are appealing to consumers from other countries, too, especially the United States, since it is the world's biggest consumer.

The Strength of Currency

Sometimes you will hear a news anchor report that the American dollar has gotten stronger. That means the dollar is worth more on the global scene when compared to the currencies of other countries. This affects a country's saving and spending, as well as yours.

There are good and bad aspects to a strong dollar. To mention one, we've seen how being a saving country brings down the value of China's prices. China likes that because U.S. consumers then favor its prices and purchase Chinese products with strong U.S. dollars. This leads China to export more goods, which means it is profiting off of America. At the time of this writing, China is exporting 40 percent of its GDP. The United States is exporting 11 percent.

Foxconn is a Chinese company that manufactures many of the latest electronics products developed by American companies, such as the Apple iPad. The Chinese can do this much more economically.

Is that bad or good for America? Well, probably both. It means America imports more goods than it exports, which is to say it buys more goods than it sells across its borders. That means Americans have a broad choice of products. Of course, that also means jobs for making these products might be relocated to other countries. If your mom just lost her job in America, it might be because the job can now be done cheaper offshore. That might very well affect your personal spending habits.

Chapter 2

The Role of Banks

What allows countries to trade with one another in products from automobiles to hockey pucks to computers? The answer is banks. Banks also provide an important safe place for you to save your extra cash and even earn some interest.

The basics of banking can get confusing, but banks really operate on a simple premise. Lots of people like you keep money in a bank savings account. The bank agrees to pay you a certain rate of interest for the use of your money. Then the bank lends out some of your money to, say, a business and charges it higher interest rates for the loan. This is how the bank makes a profit. The business benefits, too. It gets money to operate on and grow and make profits for itself. In this way, you and your savings account are directly tied into banks, business, and even world trade.

Banks can be seen as the grease that lubricates the gears of the economic engine. They are essential to keeping businesses running smoothly both domestically and internationally.

When businesses trade with each other, either in one country or across borders, many steps are involved that require the use of banks. For instance, an American automobile manufacturer must ship cars to customers in Italy. Yet suppose the price of shipping to Italy suddenly goes up. Also suppose the manufacturer runs short of cash. It will rely on banks to solve that problem. Here's how.

The FDIC

Under most conditions, savings and loan banks are quite safe. If you deposit cash in a savings and loan bank account, the federal government insures your savings for up to $250,000 through the Federal Deposit Insurance Corporation (FDIC). If the bank were to fail and not pay back the money you have deposited, the FDIC would make good on your deposits up to $250,000.

Commercial Paper

Banks offer what is called commercial paper to businesses. Commercial paper is an assurance that if financial conditions change in unexpected ways, such as unanticipated shipping charges, the bank will provide short-term loans to cover the extra costs. Commercial paper therefore ensures that product deliveries can be made and business conducted without delays.

Commercial paper offered to businesses by banks helps avoid major snags. For instance, suppose a fruit dealer ships Florida oranges to northern Canada, and it discovers that the Canadian dollar has suddenly risen in value compared to the American dollar. The price of shipping just went up. Now the fruit dealer needs extra cash in a hurry to pay for Canadian shipping before the oranges go bad. The fruit dealer can go to the bank. Commercial paper is extended by the bank, the shipping is paid for, and the fruit dealer makes plans to pay the debt at a later date.

Businesses large and small rely on bank financing to be able to continue operations on a daily basis. Time-sensitive businesses, such as farming, particularly depend on banks because of the perishability of their products.

That deposit you made in your savings account in some small yet essential way keeps the flow of oranges steady from Florida to northern Canada. Your money helps make commercial paper possible. This is how you affect trade. Also, you are affected when the bank makes profits and turns those profits around to offer your parents, say, a loan to buy the house they always wanted. You're also affected the next time you bite into a tasty orange.

The LIBOR

You might wonder, how do banks determine what rate of interest to charge for commercial paper? Considering the number of countries involved in international trade, it helps to have a single place to go for interest rates. That place is London, England. According to Nouriel Roubini in *Crisis*

When the market sours for a particular industry, such as retail, banks are less willing to take the risk of lending money to those businesses. This cuts off the lifeblood, capital, to the sector and accelerates the market downturn.

Economics, "In testament to London's enduring place in financial history, the most important rate at which money is lent is known as the London Interbank Offered Rate (LIBOR)." When a business needs commercial paper, the rate of that loan will be determined by the going rate of the LIBOR at that time.

You might also have considered a potential problem such as the following one for our fruit dealer shipping oranges: What if that shipment of oranges sat at the Canadian border, and the bank refused commercial paper needed for shipping?

That's exactly the kind of crisis many businesses faced during the Great Recession of 2006–2009. We'll see how a financial tool called leverage backfired and contributed to the dilemma.

Leverage

Prior to the Great Recession, many banks and investment firms made some bad investments. Even many top economists didn't predict the looming disaster. In fact, banks and investors were so enthusiastic and unsuspecting that they borrowed more money so that they could make even bigger investments, which turned out to be bad as well.

NOTICE TO DEPOSITORS

* * *

This bank has been closed and is in the hands of the Federal Deposit Insurance Corporation (FDIC). The FDIC is attempting to arrange for the failed institution to be merged into a healthy one. If this effort is successful, all deposits of the closed bank will be shifted to the acquiring bank and there will be little or no interruption in the provision of banking services.

If such a transaction cannot be arranged, the FDIC will move as quickly as possible either to pay depositors the amount of their deposits up to the $100,000 insurance limit, or to make insured deposits available through another area bank.

An announcement will be made as soon as possible.

* * *

FDIC

FEDERAL DEPOSIT INSURANCE CORPORATION

While banks, just like any business, can make bad financial decisions and be forced to close, the FDIC protects depositors' money to a certain amount.

When you borrow money to help make an investment larger, that borrowed money is called leverage. If all goes well with leveraging, the profits can be enormous. If all does not go well, two parties—both borrower and lender—can lose a lot of money. Leveraged investments have bigger impacts because the potential profit or loss is magnified, but so is the risk.

Moral Hazard

A secondary factor in the Great Recession was a result of what is known as "moral hazard." This is when a person grows careless when taking risks, such as investing, because he or she feels that there are no consequences to failing. Moral hazard is kind of like taking math tests in school where you're guaranteed to pass the class no matter how well or poorly you score. Since math is hard work, you'd probably take some tests where you didn't prepare at all. Your learning would suffer.

In the Great Recession, certain banks were able to make home loans to people who couldn't afford them and then pass those bad loans (for a fee) to unsuspecting customers down the line. As John Lanchester says in his book *I.O.U.*, "Why would any sane person lend money to someone with no income, job, or assets? Answer: because they were selling the loan to somebody else, so they didn't care."

In the Great Recession, the world economy began to collapse for many reasons. Now investors who had leveraged their bad investments suddenly lost their investments, plus their leveraged money. They could not pay their debts to the banks they borrowed from.

Now the banks were short of cash. It was like sparks from one fire lighting up another. Because the banks were short of cash, they couldn't lend out enough commercial paper. This resulted in businesses, which depended on commercial paper for routine financing, being turned away at the bank. Many businesses folded. In the real world, some fruit dealers watched their oranges spoil while they sat at the border.

The Great Recession may have cost your mom her job and took homes away from many other people who could no longer pay their mortgages, but it also devastated whole countries. Also hit hard were migrant workers from Mexico, Nicaragua, Guatemala, Paraguay, Ecuador, and the Philippines, who would normally send their earnings back home to bolster those economies. These struggling countries lost much of their income. Their economies were devastated.

Then in 2008 the whole country of Iceland faced economic disaster. Its banks had no money due to mismanagement and the deepening world recession. So what is considered safe with spending and saving? Should everybody keep their money under the mattress until they need it? Would that be safer and wiser?

The answer is no. Investing is generally a good use of money, but caution is necessary. As Arthur Simon suggests in his book *How Much Is Enough?*, "While free enterprise may be a remarkable engine for driving economic growth, an engine is not the same as a steering wheel." In other words, some regulation might be necessary before our economy engine gets headed for the ditch.

A Changing Economic World

Meanwhile, the world economic superpower order is shifting. In past years, the major economies were those of the United States, Japan, Germany, France, the United Kingdom, Canada, and Italy. Now Brazil, Russia, India, and China, known as the BRIC countries, have become economic powerhouses themselves.

Your personal spending and saving will no doubt result in goods and services purchased from these countries in the coming years.

Chapter 3

When to Spend and When to Save

One occasion requiring caution and education is when you make the biggest purchase of your life. That is, when you buy a house. Let's say you are now grown, married, and have two children. They all depend on you. You and your spouse decide the time is right to buy a house. Your family carefully prepared for this big decision by saving money. You went out to dinner only once a month for several years so that you could deposit the money into a savings account. You wanted a new car, too, but you got the old one fixed instead, even though it shows a dent from when your spouse backed into a pole and your kids tell you that it's embarrassing when other kids see the dent. You felt pressured to buy a new car, but you held out. You were thinking, just wait until the kids see their new bedrooms.

Now you approach a real estate broker and figure out that your savings are finally enough for a down payment, but you'll need more than just your savings. A *lot* more. That's where the bank comes in.

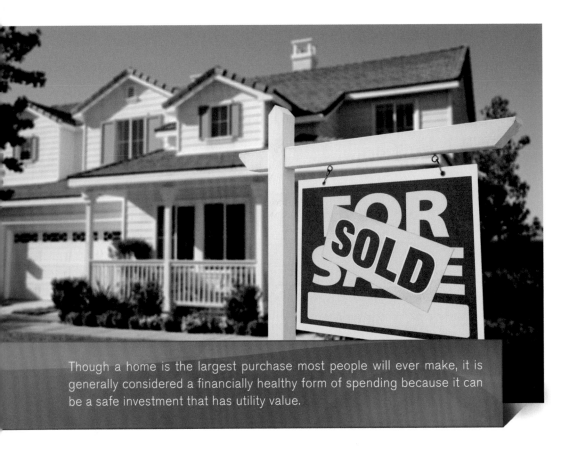

Though a home is the largest purchase most people will ever make, it is generally considered a financially healthy form of spending because it can be a safe investment that has utility value.

You find your dream home. You make a price offer to the current owners of the house, and they agree to sell it to you. Your kids are all excited. Your bank agrees to a home mortgage loan. Soon you will commit to the mortgage terms.

That night, you break out into a cold sweat. You ask yourself, "What am I getting into?" Your savings aren't nearly enough to pay for a whole house. You will be taking out that huge mortgage. With that comes a big risk. You've been through it a million times in your mind, but before you sign on the dotted line, you and your spouse want to be as certain as possible that you can afford this.

How Mortgages Work

How the mortgage works is this: your down payment from savings, plus the bank mortgage money you borrow, is all paid to the owner of the new home. You also pay some fees for lawyers, taxes, public records, and a survey of your property lines. When you sign for the mortgage loan, you agree to repay the bank monthly installments on the mortgage. Each monthly payment will include the interest on the loan, too. Typically, you will make a loan payment every month for thirty years, though most people sell their homes before then. When the home is sold, the mortgage is paid back when the seller receives payment.

Collateral is some item that the bank can take back if you fail to pay back your loan. With home loans, the house is normally the collateral. If you don't make your monthly payment, you are said to be in "default." The bank now has the right to take away its collateral (your home), sell it, and give you whatever is left over. You would also be forced to leave the home.

Your mortgage is called a long-term loan. That's different than the commercial paper we considered in the last chapter, where businesses take short-term loans to get through routine business fluctuations. Both kinds of loans, however, must be paid back in a timely fashion or the borrower is in default and must forfeit whatever collateral has been put up.

As mentioned, interest rates will become a significant part of your monthly mortgage payment. Who determines those interest rates in America is the U.S. Federal Reserve Bank. It is the central bank of America. Often referred to as just "the Fed," the Federal Reserve Bank is part of the American

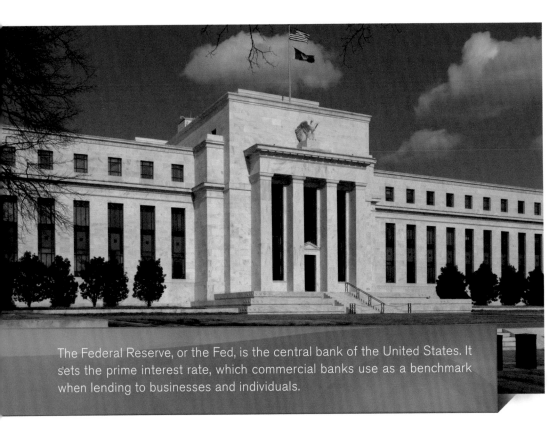

The Federal Reserve, or the Fed, is the central bank of the United States. It sets the prime interest rate, which commercial banks use as a benchmark when lending to businesses and individuals.

Federal Reserve System. It also has extremely important economic functions that affect you, your spending, and your saving in intricate ways. The Fed also has great influence on the world economy.

Since your home mortgage is a long-term loan, its interest rate has a huge impact on how much you pay each month. And since the Fed influences the interest rate for the loan, whatever that rate is when you sign for the loan will normally remain the same for you for the life of the loan. If that interest rate is currently quite high, before you buy, you and your family might very well decide to delay your home purchase until the rate comes down. Here we are facing that painful

The Role of Central Banks

All major countries have a central bank. In America, this is the Fed; in Canada, it is the Bank of Canada. You'll find information about others at the end of this book, where you can explore their Web sites to find out more about their functions, currencies, and much more.

The central bank of a country works to make sure that the economy runs smoothly. We quoted earlier from Arthur Simon's observation that the economy is a marvelous engine that is regulated by what can be viewed as a steering wheel. The central bank climbs into that driver's seat and takes control as much as it can.

Sometimes central banks of different countries operate in quite differing ways when one might instead expect the world economy to dictate one single approach. For instance, during the Great Recession, the Fed was pouring cash into the American economy to power its engine and bolster the housing market. Meanwhile, in Canada, the central bank was doing just the opposite. The Bank of Canada picked the better approach in that particular crisis.

The Fed has three specific main goals, which are to make sure the American economy has 1) maximum employment; 2) stable prices; and 3) moderate long-term interest rates, including your mortgage interest rates.

deferred gratification again. We might choose to wait for a lower interest rate.

But there are secondary considerations also. Waiting might not be a good idea either. If the price of the home you want is likely to rise a lot if you wait, it might cost you more if you buy it later. Another name tied to rising prices is "inflation."

Inflation

Inflation is a number that tells how fast prices are rising. It works like this: Let's consider a smaller example first. Suppose the price of downloading a song is $1. If the rate of inflation is 2 percent, next year your download would cost $1.02. If the rate of inflation is instead 10 percent, next year that download would cost $1.10. A higher rate of inflation means prices are rising faster.

Inflation is a general increase in prices of products such as groceries. Inflation is a natural effect of economic growth, but too much inflation could be a symptom of government overspending.

A house costs a lot more than a music download. High inflation could make a home purchase price rise by thousands of dollars. So if inflation isn't too high right now but interest rates are high, maybe you can wait until interest rates come down before you buy that house. Maybe, however, you really need a house immediately and decide it's worth the added monthly expense of higher interest rates. The decision will be yours to make based on your situation.

Keeping Interest Rates in Check

The Fed actually makes efforts to control both inflation and interest rates. Inflation is a natural occurrence in the economy. In fact, slight inflation is generally said to be desired if it remains at a maximum of 2 percent a year and a minimum of 1.7 percent. These levels of inflation are thought to stimulate growth in the economy.

One way the Fed controls inflation is through the buying and selling of bonds to American banks. Say inflation is rising too steeply, much beyond 2 percent. The Fed might control inflation in the following way. It sells bonds to the nation's banks. To buy the bonds, the banks pay cash to the Fed. The banks like this because they earn interest on the bonds. The Fed keeps this cash locked up. This means there is less cash out there in the banks and therefore less for banks to lend out. This means there is less commercial paper to offer to businesses, so commerce slows down, there's less buying and selling, and inflation is tamed. Prices rise more slowly.

In times of too little or no inflation, the Fed reverses the process. It buys back its bonds from the banks. The Fed pays cash to the banks. This means the banks have lots of cash on hand to lend out. Commercial paper is more available for the business sector. Now business picks up, companies make and sell more products, and the economy becomes more robust. Prices might tend to rise. Of course, now the risk is a resumption of higher inflation. Before inflation once again gets out of hand, the Fed again steps in to manage it.

Chapter 4

Factors That Affect Your Financial Decisions

Here's how runaway inflation affects the purchase power of your dollar. The examples here might not seem possible, but they actually happened in countries around the world where inflation at times went wild.

If suddenly the price of a cheeseburger went up to $10, you would certainly have to think twice before going out to lunch. And if an inflationary trend sent the burger price up to $20 the very next day with the news threatening yet another rise, your savings would be decimated. That $20 gift from your last birthday could be gone in one meal. Of course, prices for gas, oil, milk, and many household products might simultaneously skyrocket, meaning the purchasing power of your family's dollar would sink fast. The Fed tries to avoid that.

In conditions where inflation threatens to rise too fast, the Fed acts. It will start raising interest rates and keep

The stock market is highly sensitive to all decisions made by the Fed. A financial move has the power to send the stock market soaring or into a tailspin, which in turn could hurt the economy and influence your spending choices.

raising them until inflation slows down. The higher interest rates make it more expensive for businesses to borrow bank money for commercial paper. Then business doesn't grow as fast. The economy slows down. So do price increases and inflation.

But raising interest rates can also result in other problems. Sometimes the cure for one problem creates other problems in the form of painful side effects. One side effect is that higher interest rates usually send the stock market trending downward.

Also, higher interest rates make taking out a home mortgage cost a lot more. Here's why: $1,000 borrowed at 3 percent interest means you owe $1,030. At 10 percent interest you'd owe $1,100. If these were your monthly mortgage payments, that would mean $70 more each and every month for thirty years. That totals an extra $25,200. In fact, the actual total for a long-term loan would be much larger.

If inflation is instead cruising desirably between 1.7 and 2 percent, and other factors look good, the Fed might leave the interest rate alone. Businesses will now continue to borrow and grow, commercial paper is available, and the economy hums along. That usually means more jobs are available and perhaps your mom is able to get back that job she lost. That flat-screen television is looking like a family purchase—well, possibly anyway.

Basis Points

When the Fed changes interest rates, it does so in increments called basis points. Basis points are fractions of the difference between the Fed interest rate and the LIBOR interest rate. Recall that the Fed rate deals with interest rates in America. The LIBOR is the standard interest rate for the whole world.

Just the slightest hint of Fed action with interest rates results in a flurry of economic response across the United States and the globe. Here's how an announcement from the Fed might immediately impact you and a spending or saving decision.

Warning the Economy

Imagine one day the news anchor reports, "The Fed chairman said the Fed expects to raise interest rates by one basis point." He didn't say that he will raise the interest rate, just that he expects to. Here's why he might say that:

The Fed occasionally just suggests action it might take in the future. In this way, it hopes to influence the economy into changing before it is forced to actually act. It's kind of like a

Federal Reserve chairman Ben Bernanke is one of the most powerful people in the world. His commentary can move entire markets, both domestically and abroad, so it's critical that he choose his words carefully.

hint your mom makes about your punishment if you don't first clean up your room. She wants action before she has to act. When the Fed chairman says, "We are considering raising the interest rates," he's dropping a hint, and when he does, the whole financial world pays attention.

You might be thinking, wow, this can get confusing. It can. But you want to be successful even though you operate in a world of shifting conditions. Despite the rules about economics, the real economy often acts in unexpected ways.

Even the experts get surprised, or even shocked. Before the Great Recession, hardly any economic experts saw it coming, according to Ip in *The Little Book of Economics.* Ip says that one of the world's biggest financial newspapers, the *Wall Street Journal*, surveys about fifty professional economy forecasters each month. In 2006, not one predicted the major recession, which was then approaching. Ip adds that even professional economists often miss serious economic problems because they are looking in the wrong place.

Does this mean we should avoid learning about economics because it is sometimes unpredictable? Well, no. It's important to accept that we'll be surprised on occasion, and we'll have to react to that with the best information we have to make the right decisions.

Scams

Occasionally, fraudulent operators manage to swindle people out of their life investments. It's crucial that you be aware of all these potential distracting and criminal factors. You will always make spending and saving decisions in a sphere of some uncertainty. Scam artists are very good at deception and making their targets feel that they are in complete safety, like the fly drifting closer to the spider's innocent-looking web.

Perhaps the most notable criminal in this shady area was Bernard "Bernie" Madoff, a businessman who lured friends, family, charities, successful businesspeople, and even financial experts into his investment scheme, only to rob them all. He stole billions of dollars. He went to jail leaving the message behind that if an investment looks too good to be true, it probably is.

Interest Rates and Home Buying

Let's say you are about to buy your house. Then the chairman of the Fed appears on television and says the Fed will be lowering interest rates by several basis points. Such news might have been boring for you in the past, but now you suddenly pay attention. You connect the financial dots. If the Fed lowers rates, the bank home mortgage loan interest rates will be lower. Lower mortgage interest rates mean a lower monthly payment for you. The Fed's news might encourage you to purchase a home when the rates do drop. Maybe then you can afford that new car loan, too.

Or perhaps you might decide to take advantage of the lower Fed rates in another way. Lower Fed rates usually means the stock market will go up. Maybe you've been thinking you should invest some money in the stock market for your future. You might decide to invest a portion of your available cash right now, buying inexpensive shares of stock that might soon rise in price. Then you plan to sell them later for a profit.

Of course, with investing we can never be 100 percent certain of anything. There is risk involved, and one risk is that we might lose it all. So before you invest, you might consider how much you can stand to lose if another Great Recession hits out of nowhere and the stock market suddenly goes south.

Most investors now agree that the signs of danger were there with Madoff's scheme. But the promises of profits were so large that the investors were convinced to overlook their doubts. Temptation made these investors forget the sense

Bernard Madoff orchestrated the largest financial scam in U.S. history. He single-handedly wiped out the savings of thousands of investors, totaling billions of dollars.

of caution that's necessary whenever anyone says, "Let me manage all your money."

Risks and Rewards

Investments operate on a risk-reward economic stage. In general, the bigger the risk, the larger the financial reward. Let's start with little risk and work our way up.

If you deposit your cash in a savings and loan savings account, you will earn low interest rates but have a very safe investment. Recall that the FDIC guarantees your savings up to $250,000. With deposits in a bank savings account, you also have what are called liquid assets. "Liquid" means that some investment can quickly be converted into cash. A wallet full of $10 bills is quite liquid. A house is not a liquid investment because it might take a while to be sold and converted into spendable cash.

We've seen how bonds like U.S. Treasuries are quite safe and fairly liquid. Countries and big investors buy them to keep their cash safe and earn interest, but the price of safe investments like Treasuries is the smaller payout of interest earned. On the other hand, riskier investment such as stocks usually result in higher payoffs. But the price of a bigger payoff is the risk that the stock might drop in price.

Chapter 5

On the State Level

Imagine the governor of your state was jolted awake at 2 AM thinking, "If I can't get this budget to balance, the legislature won't accept it. And then the state police, toll bridge operators, fire fighters, hospitals, universities—everything will be shut down!"

The governor does have a concern. Her state can only spend the same amount of money that it takes in. Unlike the federal government, her state government cannot run up much debt. Also unlike the federal government, the state governor cannot print money in a pinch. This means she must balance her budget each year or risk default. Somehow she must raise billions of dollars for roads, bridges, schools, police, prisons, Medicaid, economic development, and more.

That certainly might cause someone to lose sleep at night. You might worry, too. Where would you be if the police were suddenly not on the job? Or if garbage pickup suddenly stopped? Or if your water was turned off?

In tough economic times, governors such as Chris Christie of New Jersey must lead their state to financial stability.

Operating Expenses

How the governor and her legislative branch raise the money needed for state expenditures will also impact your spending and saving. As a resident, you will benefit from state government expenses, but you will also pay for those benefits.

A natural disaster can destroy homes, farms, factories, and more. A region's economy can be devastated, with jobs and employment literally washed away, as was the case after Hurricane Katrina struck the Gulf Coast in 2005.

The state receives about one-third of its money from the federal government and gets the rest from sales taxes, income taxes, fees, tolls, and the sale of bonds.

As long as the state (or local government) income funding matches its outgoing expenses, the state can operate

State and Municipal Bonds

You might someday consider an investment in your state's bonds. The bond would pay you interest. The investment helps your money grow, and you receive the price of the bond back when you decide to cash it in, plus you keep the interest that you earn along the way. Well, except for some. Since interest is income for you, you might pay taxes on that.

You might wonder, "If I buy state or municipal bonds, how can I trust them to be there when I try to cash them in?" This is a good question. There are ratings agencies, the three biggest being Fitch, Moody's, and Standards and Poor's, which rate the economic health of countries, states, municipalities, or other large organizations selling bonds. The best rating given is AAA, and any slight deviation from this would cost the bond seller money. That's because the higher the rating, the more confident the buyer of the bond.

If a state has shown trouble in balancing its budget in the past, or if its sources of funding are in question, a rating of AAA might fall a little bit. Then buyers of bonds sold by that state will require it to pay higher interest rates to the holder of the bond. This makes it more expensive for the state to raise money by bond sales. And it means that state will have less money for services that its constituents require. Maybe it will cut some funding for schools to make up the difference. That might interfere with your college plans.

Local municipalities, like your local government, might also offer bonds to raise money for their operations, such as sewage treatment, water, conservation, parks, and other necessary local functions. Special municipal bonds, often referred to as "munis," are offered by municipalities. Munis pay lower rates of interest but are typically tax-free.

smoothly. Sometimes unforeseen expenses pop up. Then perhaps cuts in crucial services must be made.

When Funding Is Down

Disaster that strikes a state or local municipality and causes economic crisis could come from many directions and possess quite different faces. In recent years, Hurricane Katrina devastated the economies of Louisiana, Mississippi, and other states near the Gulf of Mexico. The beaches were wiped out. Buildings were wrecked. Tourism dollars, plus tax dollars that run those states, were suddenly dwindling, yet the residents needed the states' routine services and emergency services more than ever. Residents of those states lost their homes, food supplies, schools, and possessions. Many people were forced to flee the area and leave everything they owned behind to find a location with shelter, food, and safety.

Occasionally, a big economic problem comes from inside the economic system itself. In New York, the Great Recession and a sudden collapse of the housing market left the financial district of Wall Street in ruins. State taxes were reduced because people in the financial sector weren't earning large salaries anymore. The state received less money from taxes. So the state was forced to cut services to its citizens.

In California, mismanaged investments of public money and bonds left a whole county bankrupt.

When the state loses necessary funding, its services to the public suffer. And you are part of that public domain. You might not like where that takes you. And sometimes the local economic problem is not caused by local trouble. As author Ip says, "Local business and consumers could be doing fine, but if the global economy is sickly, then the U.S. exports will be weak, affecting jobs, incomes, and growth at home." Perhaps an economic failure of a computer company in Asia causes a small factory that makes batteries in a tiny U.S. town to go out of business.

A Slowing Economy

With a slow economy, we feel it at home. Beyond luxury items such as a bike, iPad, or maybe eating out once in a while, some families could find themselves hard pressed to put regular meals on the table.

If your mom has not found work yet, and your dad's firm fired him and just moved to Brazil because production costs are lower there, your family might be living on unemployment insurance payments that don't pay all the bills. Now the family budget is tight, entertainment expenses are cut, and movies on demand are no longer available because mom and dad had to cancel cable television.

The squeeze might even get worse, since the car payment is still due each month and so is the mortgage payment. It seemed so manageable before when mom and dad were working, but now they sit and talk behind closed doors like there are secrets that are always bothering them. Maybe they are wondering if they should skip their daughter's braces and even the routine dental visits for cleaning and checkups. With preventive care neglected, these skipped health care appointments may result in health problems and sickness down the road.

For a young person, perhaps a cruel reality of a slashed family clothing allowance creates a painful set of

For parents feeling the financial pinch of a tight economy, a painful decision might be to sacrifice their child's cell phone or cut allowance to keep expenses down.

circumstances. If you are worried that you don't look so good to your friends and everyone else, your confidence isn't exactly what you'd like. You know that friendships aren't made of clothing, and yet wouldn't it be nice to have stylish clothes again? But budget cuts go far beyond clothing. Perhaps a teen might be forced to defer or even forget a college education.

The Big Business of Small Business

In New York State, as reported on the state government Web site, "Small businesses are the heart of the American economy, comprising 98 percent of all businesses in New York and employing more than half of New York's private sector workforce."

As in New York, small businesses form a major

A mall filled with thriving small businesses attracts large crowds of consumers. They make purchases and stimulate the larger economy.

part of most state economies across America. This creates a healthy mind-set for young people, that is, to consider that big results can spring from small beginnings. The combination of technology and the modern ability to gain access to all kinds of information has made some young people, even teenagers, highly successful in the business world.

Small businesses are known to cause other small businesses to spring up. For instance, a local company that starts selling sandwiches to venders might provide a major boost to a neighboring company that manufactures condiments and another that sells packaging supplies. Suddenly, one little company has become three successful companies. Each pays taxes. Each contributes to the state and local economy. And somewhere in that growing number of small businesses, perhaps an opening comes up for the job your mom has been looking for, as bookkeeper for a small but successful firm. Suddenly, she envisions a future with this firm, regular vacations with the family again, and perhaps—just perhaps—that flat-screen television can once again be considered.

Meanwhile, your folks are again talking about your college career. When the economy is growing, opportunities seem to grow with it. And perhaps with some small business nearby, you have a chance at picking up a part-time job after school. Then you'll resume your spending and saving decisions again. You'll observe yet again that what goes on around you in the economic world affects your spending and saving in a big way.

In each state across America, state and local governments together spend nearly the same as the federal government spends. Much of that comes in the form of grants to foster research, discovery, technology, and innovation that will lead to new products, services, and higher employment.

This kind of stimulation has revived some localities. Some cities that suffered from the failures of established corporations in town during bad times are seeing a flurry of small businesses springing up to take their places. Yet some localities have not survived and seem to languish, unable to find a way to economic success. The effects on your spending and saving will differ radically, depending on the economy surrounding you and your family.

Chapter 6

How the Economy Affects You

You might wonder why you must pay attention to economics so early in your life. The answer is, someday you may be raising a son or daughter like yourself. And that will be expensive. According to Jean Chatzky in *Not Your Parents' Money Book*, "The Department of Agriculture estimated that child care expenses for middle-income two-parent families ranged from $11,610 to $13,480." That's per child. If you take the second figure and send that child to college, the expense now jumps to around $53,480 for the year.

So a young person like you can't expect just to arrive at family living and only then start figuring out how to manage spending and saving or how the world around you manages it. You'll be too busy then. It's wise to start thinking about it now, establishing good habits that might help you later.

A credit card or an ATM card is a great privilege but also a large responsibility. If not used wisely, it can prove to be a lot more expensive than you might have planned on.

You might begin keeping careful records of your cash. This would likely lead you to consider and then actually take action on healthy and varied forms of spending, saving, investing, and talking with your parents about things like taxes, mutual funds, credit cards, ATMs, and more. We'll also discuss some of those things here, but your parents will be an invaluable resource for information.

We'll start with keeping track of your cash, wherever your stash is located right now. You can use an uncomplicated balance sheet with two columns. This two-column accounting method is simple and has been around for many, many years. As John Lanchester says in *I.O.U.*, "There's something amazing about the fact that a method used in Venice in the thirteenth century and written down in Tuscany in the fifteenth should still be in daily use in every financial enterprise in the developed world." According to Lanchester, Luca Pacioli, a Franciscan monk and a friend of Leonardo da Vinci's, recorded this useful financial tool. Microsoft uses it, Apple uses it, so does the Fed, and so do the local bank and the mini mart down the street. You can, too.

Balance Sheets

You list two headings. The left column is labeled Assets and the right is labeled Liabilities. Your record your finances for a certain period of time, say one month. Your columns might look like this:

Assets
Gift from Aunt Mavis on birthday   **$20**
In savings account at credit union   **$115**

Cash friends owe me (Joey)	$4
U.S. savings bond (when it matures)	$50
Allowance	$15
Total	**$204**

Liabilities

Owe Carla for borrowed lunch money	$3
Buy flowers for mom's birthday	$11
Buy snacks for the week	$10
Total	**$24**

Equity	**$180**

It's called a balance sheet because the total of one column equals (or balances with) the total of the other. Assets are items you own. Liabilities are debts, items you owe or will spend. Equity is the difference between assets and liabilities. (If your liabilities total more than your assets, you will have a negative equity, which is usually represented by a number in parentheses.)

Your two-column balance sheet makes it possible to see where you stand financially for any given period of time. And once things are written down, if you see that an item like snacks is too large an expenditure, you can make adjustments.

All businesses and accounting firms use this same balance sheet, though for a company like General Motors, the asset and liability columns will each have thousands of items.

To keep track of your balance sheet electronically, you might find someone who can show you how to manage your figures on a spreadsheet or an app. Otherwise, you can use pencil and paper.

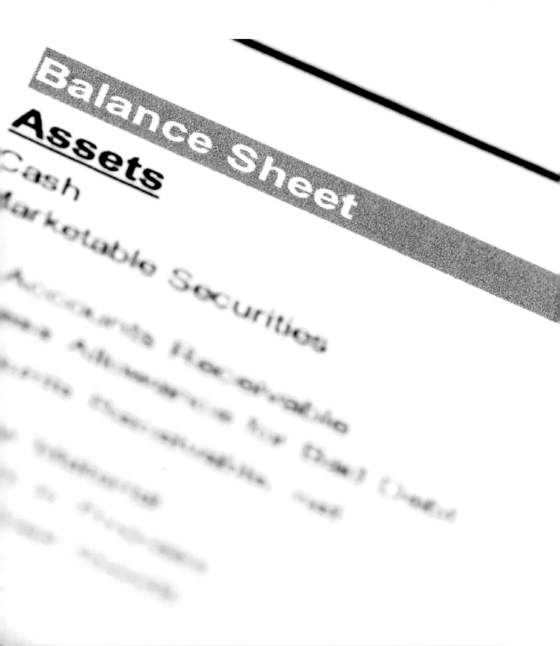

Keeping track of assets and liabilities (saving and spending) with a balance sheet helps you judge what you can afford to buy and what you need to save.

Allocating Your Assets

Once you have assessed your assets and liabilities, your equity figure will tell you the amount of cash you have available for spending and saving (unless you are in debt). Of course, the asset that's your U.S. savings bond is tied up for a few years

Learning from a Legend

You can bet that investment guru Warren Buffet used a sheet like this. He got started when he was a child. As a young newspaper delivery boy, he not only kept tabs on all income and expenses (or assets and liabilities), but he was said to have filed an income tax return with the U.S. Internal Revenue Service (IRS). He claimed his bike as an expense (liability) for his delivery service.

His equity runs into many billions of dollars. He always did his homework before investing, and still does. He's also generous. After leaving several billion to family members (when he dies), the rest will be donated to the Bill and Melinda Gates Foundation for helping less fortunate people around the world and solving huge global medical and health problems.

You, too, might decide to add a liability entry, say $3, to your liability column above and donate that $3 to a charity of your choice. That kind of spending feels good and accomplishes a lot.

until it matures; it is not a liquid asset. But that still leaves $130 in liquid assets.

First discuss with your parents ideas they might have. You might want to warn them that you are merely looking for ideas at this point. Then nobody will feel awkward if your eventual decision doesn't coincide with his or her suggestions. This is not to suggest that you wander outside restrictions they might place on your spending or saving.

Your $130 would earn interest and be safer if deposited in a bank savings account. The distance from home to the bank would also discourage impulsive spending that you'd usually soon regret anyway. Tap your bank savings only when you've decided what's next.

ATM Cards

The mere mention of an ATM card can light up a kid's eyes. How cool to get cash from a machine. The problem is, unless it's your bank's machine, you might be charged $3 for each transaction. That means you're being charged 30 percent for a $10 withdrawal. That's an extremely high rate of interest. And you can't take money out unless you have put money into the bank. There's no free cash with an ATM. ATMs are convenient for occasional cash in a hurry, but you might pay a high price for that kind of liquidity. (Recall that liquidity refers to an asset that can easily be converted into spendable cash.) Skip the ATM for now.

Credit Cards

If the ATM card looks tempting, the credit card may seem even more appealing. For the ATM card, you need to have

Before you use that ATM card to withdraw money, ask yourself whether the money is best kept in the bank. Once the money is in your hands, it's so easy to spend.

money already in the bank or else the ATM won't give you cash. With a credit card, the credit card company is offering you money that you don't have. It sounds too good to be true.

Soon, you'll be old enough for credit card companies to be sending you enticing information about what's called plastic money. Some credit cards require a regular fee just to own one. Most will let you spend money that you don't even have, but you'll have to pay it all back. There's no interest charge to you if you pay back your debt in a month. The problem is that the average credit card holder doesn't pay it back in a month. In fact, the average credit card holder builds up an enormous debt to the credit card company. That's because a brand-new knapsack is oh-so-tempting. You have to have it right now, but then a steep credit card bill comes thirty days later. Paying a debt that's a month old is like paying for a memory, especially when you have so many other ways you'd like to spend the fresh money in your pocket. So many people let their monthly payments slide into the next month. Or the next. Their balance sheets might look like this:

Assets	
Cash on hand	**$0**
Total	**$0**
Liability	
Credit card debt	**$10,000**
Total	**$10,000**
Equity	
($10,000)	

The figure in parentheses ($10,000) means that the equity is debt, a negative amount. It's money owed. Many people with credit cards have balance sheets like this from month to month, and that's only the beginning of their bad news. Owing money will now cost even more money. Each month, the debt balance of $10,000 above is charged a hefty interest fee.

A good rule to think about for the day when you consider using a credit card is this: make a pact with yourself that you will spend only an amount that you can pay back in one month. If you are not certain that you can cover your debt in a month, don't use a card at all. In fact, don't even own one until you have a full-time job.

Debit Cards

A debit card is like a credit card but with a major difference: you first must have money in a bank account. Then, say you buy a sweater at the store. You hand the clerk your debit card. The clerk swipes the card and checks your bank balance. If you have enough money in your account, that money is used to pay for the sweater. If not, you cannot buy the sweater. That's the bad news. The good news is that you are not in debt.

Deferred Gratification

Perhaps the most important rule in all economics is restraint. The hardest lesson in spending and saving is to resist temptation when you really, really want to purchase something and need to say a big fat "no" to yourself. You might want a new guitar now, or a car in the future, or a great investment opportunity many years from now, an investment that just looks too good to be true. The same rules that work for people successful in business, government, investments, and any other economic undertaking will also work for you: wait to investigate fully and calmly before you make any economic move. Patience is crucial. Deferred gratification is difficult, but it's the key to your healthy financial future. It's what saving is all about.

GLOSSARY

asset An item of value that you own, like cash, property, jewelry, or an I.O.U. from someone else.

bond A certificate of debt, normally owed along with interest to be paid at certain intervals and a certain date of maturity, when the debt will be paid back to the person holding the bond.

collateral An item offered when taking out a loan. If a loan default occurs, the collateral now belongs to the lender.

commercial paper Short-term loans from a bank to handle financial fluctuations in routine business expenses.

economics The science that deals with the production, consumption, and distribution of goods, services, and wealth.

equity The value remaining after comparing assets and liabilities. Sometimes shares of stock are referred to as equities.

export To sell goods or services to another country.

Fed rate An accepted rate of interest that the Fed charges banks for short-term loans. These rates might affect inflation, mortgage rates, car loan rates, and credit card rates of interest, and the mere Fed mention of a rate change can influence the whole economy.

Great Recession The global recession of 2006–2009.

gross domestic product (GDP) A numerical statistic used to measure the state of the economy for a country.

import To buy goods or services from another country.

inflation The rate at which prices are rising, usually given as a percent. In the United States, a healthy inflation rate is thought to be between 1.7 and 2 percent.

liability A debt, obligation, or loss of something of value to you, particularly in a balance sheet.

London Interbank Offered Rate (LIBOR) An accepted rate of interest for short-term loans that international banks charge each other.

moral hazard When a person acts irresponsibly because he or she is insured from any damage resulting from that action.

municipal bond A type of bond specifically issued by a government agency or local authority to raise capital.

profit Money gained after expenses and taxes are paid.

recession A period of slow economy, usually lasting for six months or more.

FOR MORE INFORMATION

American Bankers Association
1120 Connecticut Avenue NW
Washington, DC 20036
1-800-BANKERS (226-5377)
Web site: http://www.aba.com
The American Bankers Association provides in-depth
information on the U.S. credit and banking systems.

Bank of Canada
234 Wellington Street
Ottawa, ON K1A 0G9
Canada
(800) 303-1282
Web site: http://www.bankofcanada.ca
The Bank of Canada offers a museum and Web site
videos on monetary policy, the financial system, and
bank notes.

Board of Governors of the Federal Reserve System
20th Street and Constitution Avenue NW
Washington, DC 20551
Web site: http://www.federalreserve.gov
The Board of Governors of the Federal Reserve System
regulates monetary policy for the United States. Its
Web site has links designed for students on many
topics including credit card management, scams and
fraud, money, history, and much more.

Conference Board of Canada
255 Smyth Road
Ottawa, ON K1H 8M7
Canada
(866) 711-2262
Web site: http://www.conferenceboard.ca
The Conference Board of Canada provides insights on
    Canadian economic trends, public policy, and organi-
    zational performance.

European Central Bank
Kaiserstrasse 29
60311 Frankfurt am Main
Germany
Phone: +49 69 13 44 0
Web site: http://www.ecb.int
Information covers the euro, statistics, and monetary
    policy. It also includes video, currency exchange rates,
    and much more.

Federal Trade Commission
600 Pennsylvania Avenue NW
Washington, DC 20580
(202) 326-2222
Web site: http://www.ftc.gov
The Federal Trade Commission provides information on
    consumer rights and the laws governing credit cards
    and loans.

YoungEntrepreneur.com
Entrepreneur Media, Inc.
2445 McCabe Way, Suite 400
Irvine, CA 92614
Web site: http://www.youngentrepreneur.com
Young Entrepreneur is dedicated to providing education,
information, and networking for young entrepreneurs
who are working to launch or grow their startup businesses. The site is filled with videos, articles, links, and
information to help you learn more about being an
entrepreneur.

Web Sites

Due to the changing nature of Internet links, Rosen
Publishing has developed an online list of Web sites
related to the subject of this book. This site is updated
regularly. Please use this link to access the list:

http://www.rosenlinks.com/YEF/Save

FOR FURTHER READING

Andrews, Carolyn. *What Are Goods and Services?* New York, NY: Crabtree Publishing, 2009.

Andrews, Carolyn. *What Is Trade?* New York, NY: Crabtree Publishing, 2009.

Blatt, Jessica, and Variny Paladino. *The Teen Girl's Gotta-Have-It Guide to Money.* New York, NY: Watson-Guptill Publications, 2008.

Chatzky, Jean. *Not Your Parents' Money Book.* New York, NY: Simon & Schuster, 2010.

Cipriano, Jeri S. *How Do Mortgages, Loans, and Credit Work?* New York, NY: Crabtree Publishing, 2010.

Cohn, Jessica. *What Is Scarcity of Resources?* New York, NY: Crabtree Publishing, 2009.

Ennico, Clifford R. *The eBay Business Answer Book: The 350 Most Frequently Asked Questions About Making Big Money on eBay.* New York, NY: AMACOM, American Management Association, 2008.

Houghton, Gillian. *Creating a Budget.* New York, NY: Rosen Publishing, 2009.

Klein, Grady. *The Cartoon Introduction to Economics: Part One: Microeconomics.* New York, NY: Hill and Wang, 2010.

Klein, Grady. *The Cartoon Introduction to Economics: Part Two: Macroeconomics.* New York, NY: Hill and Wang, 2011.

Larson, Jennifer S. *Do I Need It? or Do I Want It?: Making Budget Choices.* Minneapolis, MN: Lerner Publications, 2010.

Larson, Jennifer S. *What Can You Do with Money?: Earning, Spending, and Saving.* Minneapolis, MN: Lerner Publications, 2010.

Larson, Jennifer S. *Who's Buying? Who's Selling?: Understanding Consumers and Producers.* Minneapolis, MN: Lerner Publications, 2010.

Nelson, Robin. *What Do We Buy?: A Look at Goods and Services.* Minneapolis, MN: Lerner Publications, 2010.

Rankin, Kenrya. *Start It Up: The Complete Teen Business Guide to Turning Your Passions into Pay.* San Francisco, CA: Zest, 2011.

Sowell, Thomas. *Basic Economics: A Common Sense Guide to the Economy.* New York, NY: Basic, 2007.

Thompson, Gare. *What Is Importing and Exporting?* New York, NY: Crabtree Publishing, 2010.

Thompson, Gare. *What Is Supply and Demand?* New York, NY: Crabtree Publishing, 2010.

BIBLIOGRAPHY

Bank of China. Various pages. Retrieved March 5, 2012, (http://www.boc.cn/en).

Bankrate. "Simple Savings Calculator." 2012 Retrieved March 5, 2012 (http://www.bankrate.com/calculators/savings/simple-savings-calculator.aspx).

Blatt, Jessica, and Variny Paladino. *The Teen Girl's Gotta-Have-It Guide to Money.* New York, NY: Watson-Guptill Publications, 2008.

Brookings Institution. Various pages. Retrieved March 5, 2012 (http://www.brookings.edu/opinions/2011/0907_china_currency_kroeber.aspx).

Chatzky, Jean. *Not Your Parents' Money Book.* New York, NY: Simon & Schuster, 2010.

Clemence, Sam. "The Erie Canal." 1999. Retrieved October 19, 2011 (http://www.samclemence.com/theeriecanal.htm).

International Monetary Fund. Various pages. Retrieved March 5, 2012, (http://www.imf.org/external/index.htm).

Ip, Greg. *The Little Book of Economics.* Hoboken, NJ: Wiley, 2010.

Lanchester, John. *I.O.U.* New York, NY: Simon & Schuster 2010.

LeRoy, Frank. *The Fulani Empire.* Rev. ed. London, England: Oxford University Press, 1995.

New York State Government Agencies. Various pages. Retrieved March 5, 2012, (http://www.ny.gov).

Roubini, Nouriel, and Stephen Mihm. *Crisis Economics.* New York, NY: Penguin Press, 2010.

Simon, Arthur. *How Much Is Enough?* Baker Publishing:
    Grand Rapids, MI: Baker Publishing, 2006.
St. Louis Fed Home Page. Various pages. Retrieved March
    5, 2012 (http://www.stlouisfed.org/education_
    resources/middle_school.cfm).
U. S. Department of the Treasury. Various pages. Retrieved
    March 5, 2012 (http://www.treasury.gov).
U.S. Federal Reserve Board of Governors. Various pages.
    Retrieved March 5, 2012 (http://www.federalreserve.gov).
World Bank. Various pages. Retrieved March 5, 2012,
    (http://www.worldbank.org).

INDEX

About the Author

John Strazzabosco, a retired high school math teacher, writes for young people of all ages, usually on the topic of math. Strazzabosco lives in Pittsford, New York, where he taught for thirty-three years. Recently, he has written for a math series for young adults and books on aircraft carriers and extreme temperatures for elementary math students.

Photo Credits

Cover (bottom) iofoto/Shutterstock.com; cover (ragged paper) © iStockphoto.com/Petek Arici; pp. 4-5 Yuri Arcurs/Shutterstock.com; pp. 7, 18, 29, 37, 46, 58 © iStockphoto.com/Ivan Bliznetsov; pp. 8-9 Teh Eng Koon/AFP/Getty Images; p. 10 © iStockphoto.com/John Defeo; pp. 12-13 Paul J. Richards/AFP/Getty Images; pp. 16-17 Bloomberg/Getty Images; p. 19 © Imaginechina via AP Images; p. 21 Robert Sullivan/AFP/Getty Images; pp. 22-23, 30 iStockphoto.com/Thinkstock; pp. 24-25 © Bob Daemmrich/The Image Works; p. 32 John Grant/Photographer's Choice/Getty Images: p. 34 Tom Hopkins/Aurora/Getty Images; pp. 38-39 Nelson Barnard/Getty Images; p. 41 Jewel Samad/AFP/Getty Images; p. 44 Hiroko Masuike/Getty Images; p. 47 © AP Images; p. 48 Jim Watson/AFP/Getty Images; pp. 52-53 Nancy Ney/Digital Vision/Getty Images; pp. 54-55 Dmitrijs Dmitrijevs/Shutterstock.com; pp. 59, 65 BananaStock/Thinkstock; p. 62 © iStockphoto.com/Mateusz Zagorski.

Designer: Michael Moy; Editor: Nicholas Croce;
Photo Researcher: Marty Levick